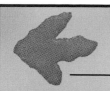

DINO STORIES

VELOCIRAPTOR

THE SPEEDY THIEF

ILLUSTRATED BY JAMES FIELD

A&C BLACK • LONDON

DINO STORIES VELOCIRAPTOR, THE SPEEDY THIEF
was produced by

David West ♋ Children's Books
7 Princeton Court
55 Felsham Road
London SW15 1AZ

Designed and written by David West
Editor: Gail Bushnell
Consultant: Steve Parker, Senior Scientific Fellow, Zoological Society of London
Photographic credits: 5t, Ty Smith; 5bl, Helen Jobson; 5br, Bob Ainsworth; 31, Fighting Dinosaur
Fossil: © American Museum of Natural History.

First published in the UK in 2007
by A&C Black Publishers Ltd
37 Soho Square
London W1D 3QZ
www.acblack.com

This book is produced using paper that is made from wood grown in managed, sustainable forests. It is natural, renewable and recyclable. The logging and manufacturing processes conform to the environmental regulations of the country of origin.

11 10 09 08 07
10 9 8 7 6 5 4 3 2 1

ISBN: 978 0 713 68618 0 (hardback)
ISBN: 978 0 713 68617 3 (paperback)

A CIP catalogue record for this book is available from the British Library

Words in bold appear in the glossary
Printed and bound in China

CONTENTS

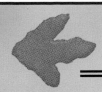 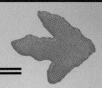

WHAT IS A VELOCIRAPTOR?

VELOCIRAPTOR MEANS SPEEDY THIEF

← *A long, stiff tail helped it to balance.*

← *Velociraptor had forward-facing eyes so it could judge distances when hunting* **prey**.

← *It had long jaws with about 80 sharp, curved teeth.*

→ *Some of its skin was probably coated in feathers to keep it warm.*

→ *Powerful legs meant it could reach speeds of 64 km/h (40 mph).*

← *It had large hands with sharp claws for gripping its prey.*

→ *It had a large, sharp claw on each foot. This was raised off the ground when it ran, to stop the claw getting blunt.*

VELOCIRAPTOR LIVED AROUND 85 TO 75 MILLION YEARS AGO, DURING THE **CRETACEOUS** PERIOD. **FOSSILS** OF ITS SKELETON HAVE BEEN FOUND IN MONGOLIA, RUSSIA AND CHINA (SEE PAGE 30).

← Adult Velociraptors measured up to 1.8 metres (5.9 ft) long, 0.62 metres (2 ft) high at the hip. They weighed 20 kg (45 lb) or perhaps even twice this amount.

FEATHERED DINOSAURS

Fossils of **ancestors** of Velociraptor show that they had feathers. Some scientists think that this dinosaur was coated in feathers to keep it warm, like feathers in a padded jacket or duvet.

HOOKED CLAW

This fossil of Velociraptor's claw is 9 cm (3.5 inches) long. It has a sharp point but does not have a sharp blade. Velociraptor used the claws like hooks, to hang on to its prey while it attacked with its teeth. The teeth had **serrated** edges, like steak knives, so they could bite through skin and muscle more easily.

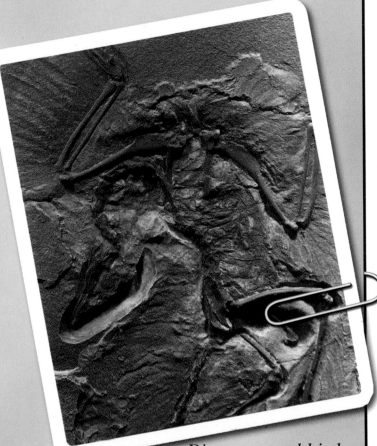

Dinosaur and bird fossils sometimes show evidence of feathers, like this Archaeopteryx.

PACK HUNTERS

Velociraptor probably lived and hunted in a pack, like **African wild dogs** do today.

MODERN ANCESTORS

The skeleton of Velociraptor is similar to the kiwi, a flightless bird living in New Zealand today. Experts think Velociraptor might have been warm-blooded like modern birds.

PART ONE... THE INVADER

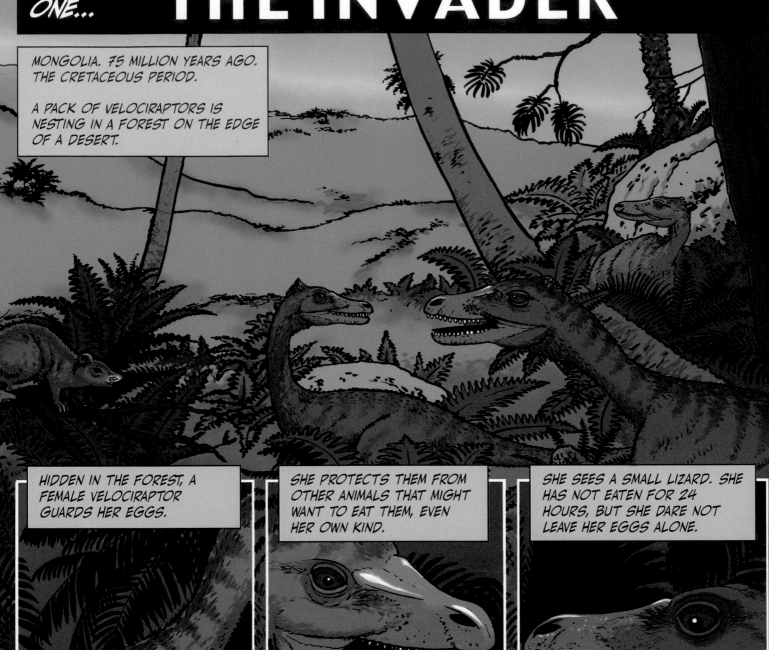

MONGOLIA. 75 MILLION YEARS AGO. THE CRETACEOUS PERIOD.

A PACK OF VELOCIRAPTORS IS NESTING IN A FOREST ON THE EDGE OF A DESERT.

HIDDEN IN THE FOREST, A FEMALE VELOCIRAPTOR GUARDS HER EGGS.

SHE PROTECTS THEM FROM OTHER ANIMALS THAT MIGHT WANT TO EAT THEM, EVEN HER OWN KIND.

SHE SEES A SMALL LIZARD. SHE HAS NOT EATEN FOR 24 HOURS, BUT SHE DARE NOT LEAVE HER EGGS ALONE.

HISSSSSSSS

SOME VELOCIRAPTORS ARE RETURNING FROM A HUNTING TRIP.

THEY HAVE NOT BEEN SUCCESSFUL. HUNGER MAKES THEM BAD-TEMPERED AND AGGRESSIVE.

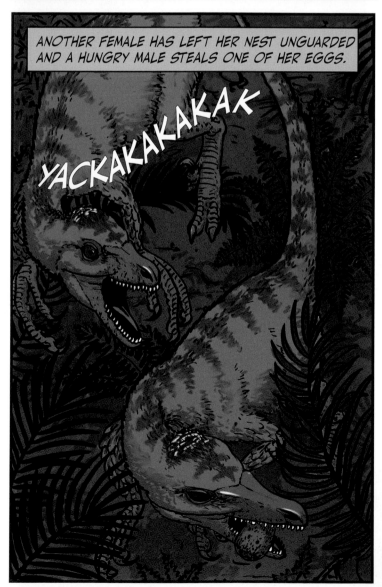

ANOTHER FEMALE HAS LEFT HER NEST UNGUARDED AND A HUNGRY MALE STEALS ONE OF HER EGGS.

THERE IS A SCUFFLE AS OTHERS JOIN IN TO FIGHT FOR THE FOOD.

THE VELOCIRAPTORS SUDDENLY STOP FIGHTING.

THEY FEEL A FAINT TREMOR THROUGH THE GROUND...

...AND ANOTHER. THE VELOCIRAPTORS HIDE.

ABOVE THEIR HEADS, GIANT CLAWS RIP AT THE BRANCHES. IT IS A THERIZINOSAURUS, A GIANT PLANT-EATING DINOSAUR.

CRACK

ALTHOUGH IT IS NOT A THREAT TO THE VELOCIRAPTORS, IT IS STEADILY HEADING IN THE DIRECTION OF THE NESTING AREA.

THE VELOCIRAPTORS TRY TO DISTRACT THE THERIZINOSAURUS.

THE THERIZINOSAURUS LOOKS DOWN ON THE VELOCIRAPTORS AND SLOWLY SWINGS ITS GIANT CLAWS AT THEM.

THE CLAWS SHAKE A SMALL MAMMAL, ZALAMBDALESTES, FROM A TREE.

TWO VELOCIRAPTORS FIGHT OVER THE FALLEN MAMMAL.

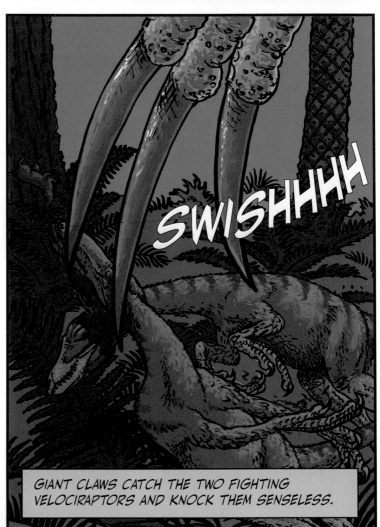

SWISHHHH

GIANT CLAWS CATCH THE TWO FIGHTING VELOCIRAPTORS AND KNOCK THEM SENSELESS.

THE VELOCIRAPTORS CONTINUE TO DISTRACT THE THERIZINOSAURUS AND EVENTUALLY IT TURNS BACK.

THE TIRED VELOCIRAPTORS RETURN TO THE NESTING SITE.

A MOTHER HEARS HER **HATCHLINGS** CALLING FROM THEIR EGGS...

KEEK

KEEK

...THE EGGS BEGIN TO CRACK...

CRICK

...EVENTUALLY, TWO MALES ARE FREE FROM THEIR EGGS. THEY ARE THE FIRST OF SEVERAL VELOCIRAPTORS TO HATCH OVER THE NEXT FEW DAYS.

KEEK

OVER THE FOLLOWING WEEKS THE HATCHLINGS STAY CLOSE TO THE NESTING SITE.

HERE THEY PRACTISE HUNTING. THEY CAPTURE INSECTS, LIZARDS AND SMALL MAMMALS.

THE TWO BROTHERS LEARN THAT THEY CATCH MORE IF THEY HUNT TOGETHER.

THEY LEARN THAT SOME THINGS ARE NOT SO GOOD TO EAT...

...AND SOME THINGS ARE GOOD TO EAT, BUT DIFFICULT TO CATCH.

THEY ALSO LEARN TO HIDE FROM DANGER BY DARTING UNDER COVER. EVEN THE ADULTS MIGHT EAT THEM.

THE BROTHERS ARE NOW OLD ENOUGH TO HUNT ON THEIR OWN. THEY HAVE SEEN A GROUP OF MONONYKUS HATCHLINGS.

THEY MUST BE CAREFUL. THEY MOVE FORWARDS SLOWLY. IF THEY GET TOO CLOSE THE MONONYKUS WILL SEE THEM AND ESCAPE.

THE USUALLY ALERT MONONYKUS DO NOT KNOW THEY ARE BEING WATCHED.

SUDDENLY, THE VELOCIRAPTORS BURST FROM THE UNDERGROWTH. THE MONONYKUS ARE TAKEN BY SURPRISE.

THE BROTHERS HOME IN ON THE SLOWEST.

THE STRUGGLE IS SHORT. THE VELOCIRAPTORS ARE SUCCESSFUL.

KRAAR

THEY HAVE NO TIME TO ENJOY THEIR MEAL THOUGH. A HUNGRY ADULT VELOCIRAPTOR HAS DISCOVERED THEM.

GRAAR

THE BROTHERS MUST LOOK ELSEWHERE FOR FOOD.

THE NEXT DAY, SEVERAL YOUNG VELOCIRAPTORS FIND A HERD OF GALLIMIMUS FEEDING ON A SWARM OF DRAGONFLIES.

THEY JOIN IN THE FEEDING FRENZY.

THE ADULTS LURK IN THE SHADOWS, WATCHING FOR A WEAK OR OLD GALLIMIMUS THEY CAN PREY ON.

SUDDENLY, AN ALIORAMUS CHARGES OUT FROM HIDING.

GRAARRR

THE GALLIMIMUS SEE THE ALIORAMUS AND SOUND A WARNING AS THEY FLEE.

HONK

THE HERD STAMPEDES. THE YOUNG VELOCIRAPTORS HAVE TO RUN FOR THEIR LIVES.

HONK

SOME MAKE IT TO THE SAFETY OF THE FOREST. OTHERS ARE NOT SO LUCKY.

HONK

A GALLIMIMUS HAS FALLEN AND BROKEN ITS NECK. THE ADULT VELOCIRAPTORS FIND IT AND FEED ON THE DEAD BODY.

THE YOUNGSTERS PATIENTLY WAIT FOR THEIR TURN, AT A SAFE DISTANCE. HUNGRY VELOCIRAPTORS ARE DANGEROUS, EVEN TO THEIR OWN KIND.

ROAR

BUT THE ALIORAMUS HAS SMELT THE BLOOD AND RETURNS TO FIND THE DEAD GALLIMIMUS.

THE VELOCIRAPTORS KNOW THEY ARE NO MATCH FOR THIS FIERCE MEAT-EATER AND RUN AWAY.

THE BROTHERS RETURN TO THE SITE OF THE SWARM OF DRAGONFLIES.

HERE, THEY SPOT BIRDS FEEDING ON THE CRUSHED BODY OF A VELOCIRAPTOR.

CAREFULLY, THEY STALK THE BIRDS.

ONE OF THEM RUSHES THE BIRDS, WHICH SCATTER INTO THE AIR TO ESCAPE FROM HIM. THE SECOND BROTHER LEAPS FROM A ROCK AND CAPTURES ONE OF THE BIRDS IN THE AIR.

THE MEAL IS EATEN IN SECONDS, FEATHERS AND ALL.

THE REPLY THEY HEAR DOES NOT SOUND FAMILIAR.

SKRAAK

SKRAA

SKRAA

SUDDENLY, A STRANGE GROUP OF VELOCIRAPTORS APPEARS.

THE BROTHERS STAND THEIR GROUND AND MAKE THREAT DISPLAYS.

HISSSS

HISSSS

THE STRANGERS BEGIN TO MOVE FORWARDS. THEY WANT TO KILL THE BROTHERS.

THE REST OF THE PACK ARRIVE JUST IN TIME.

SKREEK

SKREEK

SKREEK

SKREEK

THE STRANGERS TURN TO FACE THE NEW THREAT.

THE TWO PACKS FACE EACH OTHER, MAKING THREAT DISPLAYS.

SKREEK

SKREEK

THE STRANGERS ARE OUTNUMBERED...

SKRAAK

SKRAAK

SKREEK

...AND DECIDE TO RETREAT INTO THE FOREST.

SKREEK

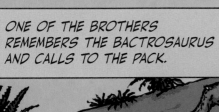
ONE OF THE BROTHERS REMEMBERS THE BACTROSAURUS AND CALLS TO THE PACK.

SKREK SKREK

THE PACK FOLLOWS THE BROTHERS TO A RIDGE.

LOOKING DOWN FROM THE RIDGE, THEY SEE THE OLD BACTROSAURUS WALKING ACROSS THE PLAIN.

THE PACK RACE DOWN THE SLOPE TO CATCH THE OLD BACTROSAURUS.

THEY LEAP ON TO HIS BACK AND NECK, CLINGING WITH THEIR SHARP-CLAWED HANDS AND THE **RETRACTABLE** CLAW ON THEIR HIND LEGS. THEN THEY BITE WITH THEIR RAZOR-SHARP TEETH.

DRAARGH

THE BACTROSAURUS IS TOO OLD AND WEAK TO PUT UP A FIGHT. HE SOON DIES FROM LOSS OF BLOOD.

THE PACK EAT QUICKLY. THERE ARE PLENTY OF LARGER PREDATORS WHO COULD EASILY STEAL THEIR MEAL.

AN OVIRAPTOR LOOKS ON. IT KEEPS A SAFE DISTANCE. THE OVIRAPTOR IS NO MATCH AGAINST A PACK OF VELOCIRAPTORS.

THE VELOCIRAPTORS DEPART. A TYRANNOSAURUS BATAAR SMELLS THE CARCASS AND COMES TO FEED ON THE LEFTOVERS.

PART FOUR

THE STORM

THE BROTHERS ARE OUT HUNTING WITH THE PACK AGAIN, IN THE DESERT. A CLAP OF THUNDER PROMISES MUCH-NEEDED RAIN.

CRACK

RUMBLE

RUMBLE

FROM A DRY GULLY ON THE EDGE OF THE DESERT, THE TWO BROTHERS WATCH A PROTOCERATOPS' NESTING SITE.

A SMALL MONITOR LIZARD TRIES TO STEAL AN EGG...

...BUT THE MOTHER CHASES IT AWAY.

THE LIZARD RUNS PAST THE TWO BROTHERS BUT THEY TAKE NO NOTICE. THEY ARE MORE INTERESTED IN A PROTOCERATOPS AT THE EDGE OF THE NESTING SITE.

THE APPROACHING STORM IS MAKING THE PROTOCERATOPS NERVOUS.

RUMBLE

WHUURK

AS THE BROTHERS WATCH, THE REST OF THE VELOCIRAPTOR PACK CREEP ROUND TO THE OTHER SIDE OF THE NESTING SITE.

THE SKIES OPEN AND RAIN LASHES DOWN. THE BROTHERS ATTACK. THE REST OF THE PACK WAIT IN AMBUSH.

WHAARK

WHAARK

WHAARK

THE PROTOCERATOPS FLEE IN ALL DIRECTIONS.

VISIBILITY IS POOR AND THE BROTHERS LOSE SIGHT OF EACH OTHER AND THEIR PREY.

ONE OF THE BROTHERS PASSES A NEST FULL OF EGGS AND FORGETS ABOUT THE HUNT.

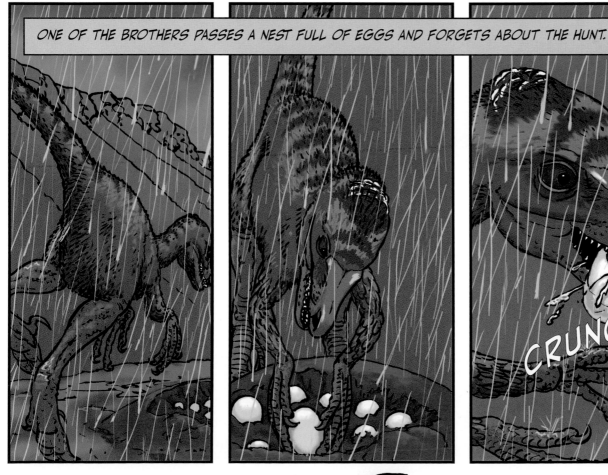

THE NOISE OF THE STORM PREVENTS THE VELOCIRAPTOR FROM HEARING THE RETURNING PROTOCERATOPS MOTHER.

SHE CHARGES AND CATCHES THE BROTHER IN THE CHEST.

HAARGH

HE TURNS TO FIGHT HER, SINKING HIS CLAWS INTO HER NECK.

SKREEEK

WHAARK

ABOVE THEM, THE RAIN HAS MADE THE SAND BANK UNSTABLE.

CREEK

SKREEEK

WHAARK

SUDDENLY, THE BANK COLLAPSES. THEY ARE BOTH KILLED INSTANTLY.

WHUMP!

THE SURVIVING BROTHER AND THE REST OF THE PACK HAVE KILLED A PROTOCERATOPS AND ARE FEEDING ON IT IN THE RAIN.

THE SURVIVING BROTHER LOOKS UP. HE REALISES HIS BROTHER IS MISSING, BUT HUNGER KEEPS HIM FEEDING.

THE PACK HEAD OFF TO DIGEST THEIR MEAL IN SAFETY. THEY STOP BY THE GULLY, WHICH IS NOW A RAGING TORRENT. THE SURVIVING BROTHER WATCHES A HERD OF PRENOCEPHALE IN THE DISTANCE, BROWSING ON SHRUBS. FOR THE TIME BEING, HE DOES NOT FEEL HUNGER. THE RAIN HAS STOPPED AND THE SUN IS WARM ON HIS BACK. AT LAST HE CAN REST FOR A WHILE.

FOSSIL EVIDENCE

WE HAVE A GOOD IDEA WHAT DINOSAURS MAY HAVE LOOKED LIKE FROM STUDYING THEIR FOSSIL REMAINS. FOSSILS ARE FORMED WHEN THE HARD PARTS OF AN ANIMAL OR PLANT BECOME BURIED AND THEN TURN TO ROCK OVER MILLIONS OF YEARS.

One of the most amazing dinosaur fossils ever found was dug up in 1971 in Mongolia. It shows a fight between a Protoceratops and a Velociraptor. The Protoceratops bites the Velociraptor's arm as the Velociraptor strikes back at its throat with the claw on its left leg.

To be caught in this pose, scientists believe the dinosaurs died instantly. A collapsing sand dune is one likely reason. A large amount of wet sand falling on the two dinosaurs would set like concrete, and preserve their pose, as seen today (below).

DINOSAUR GALLERY

ALL THESE DINOSAURS APPEAR IN THE STORY.

Mononykus
'Single claw'
Length: 1 m (3 ft)
A small, bird-like dinosaur with a single claw on each stubby arm.

Protoceratops
'First horned face'
Length: 2 m (7 ft)
A medium sized plant-eater with a large armoured neck frill.

Oviraptor
'Egg thief'
Length: 1.8 m (6 ft)
A bird-like dinosaur with a parrot-like beaked mouth.

Prenocephale
'Sloping head'
Length: 2.5 m (8 ft)
A small, dome-headed plant-eater.

Gallimimus
'Fowl mimic'
Length: 6 m (20 ft)
A large, ostrich-like dinosaur with a beak-like mouth.

Bactrosaurus
'Club-spined lizard'
Length: 6 m (20 ft)
A plant-eater of the duck-billed dinosaur or hadrosaur type.

Tyrannosaurus bataar
'Tyrant lizard of bataar'
Length: 13 m (40 ft)
A large meat-eater, weighing 4,550 kilos (5 tons).

Alioramus
'Different branch'
Length: 6 m (20 ft)
A smallish tyrannosaur, weighing 910 kilos (1 ton).

Therizinosaurus
'Scythe lizard'
Length: 12 m (39 ft)
A giant plant-eater with long finger claws.

GLOSSARY

African wild dogs Wild dogs that live in packs on the African grasslands. Their main prey is Impala, a type of buck.

ancestor Earlier type of animal from which a later animal evolved.

Cretaceous period The period of time between 146 million and 65 million years ago.

fossils The remains of living things that have turned to rock.

hatchlings Young animals that have hatched from eggs.

prey Animals that are hunted for food by another animal.

retractable Something that can be drawn back.

serrated Having a jagged toothed edge, like a saw.

INDEX